THE POWER OF POSITIVE TOUCH

Let's make positive touch travel around the world like a butterfly!

Marija Kisieliene

THE POWER OF POSITIVE TOUCH
Let's make positive touch travel around the world like a butterfly!

© 2020 Marija Kisieliene

All rights reserved. No part of this book may be reproduced, stored in a retrieval system or transmitted in any form or by any means (electronic, mechanical, photocopy, recording, scanning or other) except for brief quotations in critical reviews and articles, without the prior written permission of the publisher.

ISBN: 9798685183163

The strategies in this book are presented primarily for enjoyment and educational purposes. The information and resources provided in this book are based upon the author's personal experience and professional expertise. Any outcome is based on the author's experience and there is no guarantee that your experience will be the same or that you will have similar results.

Although the author and publisher have made every effort to ensure that the information in this book was correct at press time, the author and publisher do not assume and hereby disclaim any liability to any party for any personal or professional loss, damage or disruption caused by errors or omissions, whether such errors or omissions result from negligence, accident, or any other cause.

This book is not intended as a substitute for the medical advice of physicians. The reader should regularly consult a physician in matters relating to his/her health and particularly with respect to any symptoms that may require diagnosis or medical attention.

The author reserves the right to make changes at any time.

To my children, Naglis and Tiyanna

Table of Contents

Acknowledgements	1
Why I Wrote This Book	2
Who Is This Book For?	9
Chapter One: What is Positive Touch?	12
Chapter Two: Touch Therapies	27
Chapter Three: The 5 P's of Paediatric Massage	42
Chapter Four: Positive Touch Through Massage for Children with Special Needs	56
Chapter Five: Massage for Underserved and Abused Children	69
Chapter Six: Preparation for Massaging Abuse Survivors	87
Final Words	100

The Power Of Positive Touch

Acknowledgements

I would like to express my eternal gratitude to my business mentors James Nicholson and Jessen James,

To Kim for being the igniter of this book,

To Dea for her support in marketing and publishing this book,

To Suzanne for healing wounds deeply buried in me,

To all my friends and family who have kept me going on my journey,

And last but certainly not least, to my children Naglis and Tiyanna for their patience with me in my continued endeavour to be a better mother.

Marija Kisieliene

Why I Wrote This Book

As a massage therapist who has been in the industry for several years, I've helped numerous people with a vast variety of physical ailments. From sciatica and repetitive strain injury to rotator cuff and chronic illnesses- I've dealt with them all.

With my experience comes lessons, and one of the most important I've learned is that often, the totality of a client's pain surpasses the physical.

Their conditions bring them so much stress that as they share their heartaches while I knead their muscles, I become more than just a masseuse. I become their confidant - their friend.

The Power Of Positive Touch

That was the case with the teacher who set the momentum going for the inception of this book.

One day, she hobbled into my spa, writhing from her back pain. I could tell with one look that she was a teacher. If she were working with young children, that would explain her condition.

I have two of my own - a girl and a boy - and I know first-hand that it's no easy task to pick up after them.

Once prepped and ready for her massage, she surprised me with the loving way she talked about her students. Whereas other clients would've explained how they got the injury and complained, she went on and on about special needs children and how positive touch is essential to their development.

Marija Kisieliene

It soon became clear to me that what pained her most was not her back, but the depravity of touch her students experienced as a result of her injury.

It frustrated her to not be able to pick up a five-year-old boy with autism and establish herself as a loving figure that he can rely on.

Her desire to recover quickly led her to me, and I addressed her back issue to the best of my abilities. Eventually, she got better, and she returned to the spa with an astounding report: she could now pick up the boy.

As she was narrating this good news to me, I was struck by the significance she put on *touch*.

The Power Of Positive Touch

Touch is my profession. I've been helping people relieve tension and recover from all kinds of conditions using my hands. And yet it felt like the first time I understood that *touch* is essential, not optional.

The longer I pondered on this, the greater the pull I felt towards my own experience with touch growing up.

My parents had been abusive. They introduced touch to me as a means to demean and to control. The worst thing about this may be the fact that in spite of my repulsion to it, I became a reflection of them in my own motherhood.

What they did to me, I did to my son. There was a time when he was just a boy that I couldn't pick him up and give him the affection he deserved. I never experienced that, and I didn't know how to give it to him.

I knew deep inside, though, that he needed me to change. It was gut-wrenching for me to see him communicate that through the fear in his eyes. My parents had scarred me for life, and I couldn't watch my son suffer the same way I did.

One day, I decided that enough was enough.

The abuse in my family stops with me.

As with all lasting journeys to change, I started by educating myself with what I'd gone through; how I was mirroring it with my son, and how I could stop. Name a self-help or personal development book that even remotely discusses the subject, and I've probably read it in the past couple of years.

The Power Of Positive Touch

My knowledge about positive touch, as well as my own experiences with it in bettering my family, had built up and culminated in that encounter with the special needs teacher.

Her heart and her story sparked my eagerness to let more people know about the importance of touch to all kinds of children. Ever since, I've been doing my research, reflecting on my experiences, and polishing my skills as a professional masseuse-all to deliver this book to you.

It has not been easy getting here, and if I'm being totally honest, fear still sneaks up on me whenever my son and I embrace. The memory of the pain I experienced and consequently inflicted still returns to me with each physical contact.

Marija Kisieliene

My saving grace is his unconditional forgiveness. As part of my commitment to him to be a better mother, I've decided to make it my life goal to educate parents and teachers alike about the transformative and healing power of positive touch.

The Power Of Positive Touch

Who Is This Book For?

This book is for everyone who seeks to understand the power of positive touch.

If you picked this up, it means there's something about it you're curious to discover or to comprehend. Perhaps that's because you've never experienced it yourself, and you realize its significance in raising your own children or dealing with those you teach in school.

While this book is available to everyone, it was written primarily for parents and teachers. If you fall under either or both of those categories, I urge you to read this from start to finish.

Take out a pen and a highlighter. Write on the margins of each page. Reflect on the role touch plays in your relationship with the children in your life.

Has your touch been positive? Have you used it as a tool to affirm their worth? Do they have better self-esteem because of it?

I want you to understand the value of the physical contact you have with your children and, if you're a special needs teacher, the healing properties it can have on them.

Above all, my goal is to make this book the cornerstone of many children's recovery and passage into becoming confident and secure adults; the kind that appreciate positive touch and share it with others.

The Power Of Positive Touch

But I can't do that without your cooperation. While this book starts the momentum, it's your job to take action and to pass on the message.

It's my wish for the message of this book to reach the rest of the world. Like a butterfly that touches flowers with its gentleness and spreads its pollen, I want it to go from one family to another to help every child experience the wonders of positive touch.

Marija Kisieliene

Chapter One

What is Positive Touch?

The first sense that you developed as a foetus was touch.

Within three weeks of conception, your primitive nervous system matured. As you reached your sixteenth week, you became sensitive to sensations in all parts of your body. At twenty-five weeks, your nervous system could give pain signals to the brain. On full term, you had a fully developed sense of touch.

The Power Of Positive Touch

Even before you were aware of this, you've been conveying your emotions nonverbally. Seventy percent of your communication happens through body language, and touch amplifies it.

It's an intrinsic part of your natural design.

Different people do this in different ways. It depends on the associations built around touch during their formative years.

If you grew up in a family of huggers, it's not unusual for you to prefer a quick hug to a handshake when greeting others. On the flipside, if the people who raised you were conscious of their personal space, a hug will likely alarm you.

Your preferences when it comes to touch sprouted from your subconscious and have been evolving ever since.

Now you're at a point where you could be shaping a child's perception of it.

So, while touch is intrinsic, its effects are hardly possible to maximize through intuition alone.

Knowing all these, it's natural for you to feel that you have to be more intentional with your interactions with children.

That's good. I want you to realize as early as now that you need to be purposeful. You must remember, though, that intention loses its power when it's not backed by direction, and you can only gain direction by answering this question: How, exactly, should children be touched?

The Power Of Positive Touch

Defining Positive Touch

Positive Touch is an actual technique based on Dr. Frederick Leboyer's book *Loving Hands*. In it, he narrates how an Indian mother massages her baby while in the streets of Kolkata (formerly Calcutta).

Its name is meant to reflect a family-centred and developmentally sensitive approach to the massage of infants.

On a non-technical level, positive touch is a tool you can reach for to comfort and uplift children. When a touch is successful in evoking pleasant emotions, it's considered a positive touch.

For instance, mothers can ease their children's pain through the *appropriate* physical contact. I emphasize the word "appropriate" because what is suitable to an infant might not be suitable to an older child. Mindfulness and respect are important, even when your intentions are good.

You also have to be careful when you provide comfort through touch while children are battling negative emotions. They can unconsciously associate or "anchor" those feelings with that touch. This means that if you hug them the same way when they're in a positive state, it may trigger a negative emotion.

You can avoid this by either waiting for them to regain their composure before you hug them, or by hugging them differently. In doing this, you give them different anchors to different emotions.

The Power Of Positive Touch

Just as adults derive emotional support from touch, so do children. They're even more significant to them because they're only beginning to experience the world. This makes it critical that they anchor your touch to positive thoughts and emotions.

Positive touch aims to help children feel safe, relaxed, calm, and comforted. Used wisely and strategically, it can promote healing as well for those who need it.

The Dangers of Touch Deprivation

The absence of positive touch can lead to grave consequences. These consequences, in fact, have become so commonplace in society that many remedies have been presented to both households and educational institutions to address them.

Marija Kisieliene

Resources are available to parents and guardians on how to raise children so that they don't turn into unmanageable adults. Many have even mastered and implemented these methods to a tee.

Sometimes, though, the problem lies deeper than the words you say and the things you give.

The specific issue of touch is something you do on a subconscious level most of the time. This means you're affecting children in ways you may not be aware of.

It's not natural for you to kiss them goodnight, so you don't. You're afraid you'll drop your baby girl, so you just watch her inside her crib. Maybe you've grown up with a mindset that touch makes for fragile adults.

The Power Of Positive Touch

Now that you have your own children, you condition them that clinging to you is a sign of weakness.

Simply put, you could be doing everything else correctly, but if you don't provide this particular need for positive touch, you could be depriving them of their basic physical, mental, and emotional needs.

The information I present here has verifiable scientific backing. They prove the dangers of touch deprivation from infancy up to the latter stages of child development.

Psychologist Harry Harlow's famous experiment with rhesus monkeys became a precedent in the study of touch. Through it, he demonstrated its significance from an early age.

Marija Kisieliene

In his experiment, he took new-born rhesus monkeys from their natural mothers and placed them with two "surrogate" mothers. This gave the monkeys a choice. They can either go to the one made of wire that supplied nourishment through a baby bottle, or the other made of soft terrycloth that gave them no food.

Harlow observed that the monkey went to the wire mother only to feed from the bottle. It spent most of its time with the cloth mother.

American cultural anthropologist Margaret Mead, on the other hand, noted in her research the issues that children deprived of touch suffer from later in life.

Her work reveals that cultures that avoid physical affection in infant years have a high percentage of adult violence. Societies that indulge in a lot of touch stimulation, however, have fewer recorded instances of the same issue.

Nearly one in every three clinical referrals of children who are emotionally disturbed, hyperactive, or aggressive were deprived of touch in their earlier years.

Health Scientist James W. Prescott asserts that touch deprivation in early childhood leads to neurological dysfunction. It also gives them a higher susceptibility for drug and alcohol abuse in their adult years.

Scientists have received evidence that babies who are left in cots have 20 percent smaller brains compared to kids who are picked up more often (given that both groups of babies received proper nutrition and hygiene).

These findings are congruent with other discoveries that verify the negative effects of touch deprivation on brain development.

These kids often have low levels of serotonin, which is a neurotransmitter of the brain. It's sometimes called the "happiness hormone."

Serotonin is responsible for stabilizing a person's mood. It aids in sleep, digestion, bone health, bowel movement, and blood clotting, among other things.

Low serotonin levels can make children prone to depression, aggressive behaviour, anxiety, obsessive-compulsive disorder, and mood swings. Babies with a severe lack of it can suffer from sudden infant death syndrome (SIDS).

The Power Of Positive Touch

Brain development is also affected by other neurochemicals like cortisol, which is the stress hormone. Babies deprived of physical contact continuously produce high levels of cortisol.

Chronically elevated cortisol levels in infants are linked to brain damage. This leads to acute responses to stress throughout their lives. Such responses include increased heart rate and blood pressure. They may also have difficulty controlling their emotions and behaviour.

This aligns with a finding in the 1920s which states that infants and kids who did not experience affectionate touch in their orphanages had stunted growth.

Touch deprivation can inhibit the release of essential growth hormones. This affects the development of the brain, heart, and liver. It can also result in low production of hormones like insulin, which then leads to poor weight gain.

Other undesirable effects include the probability of these children being deceitful. Infants who are deprived of touch under one year of age may develop a propensity for lying.

As they grow older, they can also develop eating disorders and problematic behaviours. They may hug their arms and legs excessively and become too compliant or submissive. Any activity that makes up for that feeling of lack can entice them. This may then lead to reckless behaviour in an attempt to address an issue they're not even aware they have.

The Power Of Positive Touch

Touch works like medicine. All these aforementioned effects of touch deprivation can be avoided through positive touch.

Now more than ever, parents are vigilant with their children to protect them from all forms of abuse. It's an ongoing movement around the world that aims to raise safe, healthy, and well-rounded children regardless of race and background.

Since abuse is such a huge concern, it's understandable why some parents avoid all kinds of intimacy with their babies altogether.

Many teachers and caregivers also face the dilemma of gauging the extent of the physical affection they can give. Hugs, cuddles, holding hands, picking up children if they fall- all these actions are open to misinterpretation.

In this fight to end abuse, it's my wish to inspire you to give your children the positive touch they need.

Children need positive touch the moment they enter this world. If they don't get it, they may participate in unhealthy or even dangerous activities.

The solution, therefore, is to learn the proper way to incorporate positive touch at home and in schools. That's what we're going to discuss in the succeeding chapters.

Chapter Two

Touch Therapies

Touch therapy is the umbrella term for techniques that use physical contact and manipulations to promote wellbeing. It's been practiced in different cultures for thousands of years, and now modern medicine acknowledges its therapeutic effects.

Massage is the mainstream technique in touch therapies and one that can be applied to varying results, depending on expertise. It's the primary way to be intentional with positive touch, especially with children.

Marija Kisieliene

Someone may have already recommended this to you if your child ever suffered from constipation, colic, or breathing problems. Regular massage can ease their symptoms and speed up their recovery.

You may have come across stories of others massaging babies who have feeding disorders, because stimulating the nerves that help digestion can restore them to good health.

Maternity nurse and parenting expert Lisa Clegg attest that massage is a good way to relax babies. She says that signing up for local classes is beneficial not only for them, but also for you as a parent or as a caregiver.

While there's a lot of emphasis on infants when it comes to paediatric massage, we shouldn't overlook its value to older children.

The Power Of Positive Touch

Professional massage therapists, as well as parents and caregivers who have sufficient training, can help children with tension, pain, anxiety, and nausea.

While it's not, by itself, a cure, it's proven to be efficient in aiding children in their journey towards a higher level of physical, mental, and emotional relief.

As we enter a thorough discussion of its benefits, I want you to make a mental list of which issues-whether acute or chronic-apply to the children under your care. This will help you make better use of the knowledge you'll glean in this book to address these issues the next time they come up.

The Benefits of Positive Touch Through Massage

If you're caring for infants as of this reading, you're in a position to provide them with a positive touch that will merit them well into adulthood.

Massage promotes better muscle movement by enhancing their blood circulation. This is especially important in babies because the blood circulation system in their limbs is not fully developed. They also don't have sufficient mobility yet to stimulate it on their own. When blood flow to their hands and feet increase, so do their physical growth and development.

As mentioned at the beginning of this chapter, massage helps in dealing with colic and gas symptoms. Now let's discuss how.

The Power Of Positive Touch

Babies suffering from these conditions experience pain levels that make them difficult to soothe. This results in heightened stress not only for the baby, but for you as well. It's likely for you to make poor decisions in a distressed state, and for your baby to have an unsatisfactory response to other treatments.

With the use of suitable techniques, regular massage can ease their discomfort. It may even lessen the need for medication.

I recommend placing your palm flat on your baby's tummy and using a clockwise circular motion. If you prefer something gentler, use your fingertips instead. Other alternatives include drawing the letter 'n' on the tummy and bending the knees to the chest.

A domino effect starts once you make massage a part of your daily routine with your baby. You'll notice that they may sleep better, cry less, and are more alert when awake.

These benefits can then result in reduced stress for the both of you. Reduced stress, in turn, may lead to better feeding patterns, improved response to growing pains, and decreased teething pain.

Bonding with babies through massage can have wonderful effects on their respiratory health. It boosts the oxygen and nutrient flow to the cells, which then improves the condition of their lungs and their breathing patterns.

Just as touch deprivation impedes the release of growth hormones, positive touch through massage increases them to promote weight gain and better intellectual development.

The Power Of Positive Touch

Moreover, it can prompt the release of oxytocin, which is also called the "bonding hormone." This enhances your parent-child attachment and the baby's social-emotional adjustment

According to some psychologists, babies desire physical affection in an attempt to recreate the conditions of the mother's womb. This is why we have popular techniques that imitate that environment, such as skin-to-skin contact, bathing, and hand containment. You can also cuddle the baby to make them feel like they are being rocked in the womb's amniotic fluid.

Swaddling them in a blanket, which is a standard practice in modern day baby care units, also creates a snug, protective, and warm environment that they like.

Children with ADHD and autism benefit from deep pressure techniques like rolling up in a sleeping bag or a gym mat, which activates a relaxing reflex.

Majority of these benefits are carried on in the latter years of their childhood.

Touch, according to studies conducted by Pirkko Routasalo and Arja Isola, is a significant part of human behaviour from a person's birth until his death.

This means that if, right now, you're raising toddlers and even grade schoolers- don't worry. It's not too late for them to experience the benefits of positive touch. In fact, there will never be a point in their lives that it will lose its value.

The Power Of Positive Touch

In the same way that massage helps adults deal with stress, so a few minutes of it can ease a child's pain, depression, anxiety, and other emotional and physical strains.

Massage achieves this primarily by triggering the production of serotonin, endorphin, and dopamine. Each of these "positive hormones" conduct multiple tasks in the brain and in the body that can give a child an overall sense of well-being.

Since we've tackled serotonin in the previous chapter, let's focus on endorphin and dopamine.

Endorphins are the body's pain reliever. Reward-producing activities such as exercising, laughing, eating, and getting a massage boosts this, and therefore alleviates discomfort. It's the body's natural way to cope with pain.

Low levels of endorphins make children susceptible to depression, chronic headaches, anxiety, sleep problems, impulsive behaviour, and moodiness.

Dopamine, on the other hand, is dubbed as the "feel good" neurotransmitter that is produced when there's an expectation of a reward. When children associate massage with pleasure, even the anticipation of having one after a stressful day at school is enough to release dopamine.

While it's commonly known for that particular role, it's worth noting that it aids in many more physiological activities such as digestion, focus, memory, and kidney and heart function.

The Power Of Positive Touch

Apart from triggering these hormones, the increase in blood flow that massage induces helps in improving tissue elasticity. When tissues are more elastic, they're more resistant to the formation of muscular knots. Fewer knots mean lesser stress.

Giving children a massage is a great way to enhance your communication with them through bonding. They can perceive it as your acknowledgement of the challenges they're facing. That's important to them because they do need their problems and feelings to be validated and addressed, regardless if they seem trivial to your adult worldview.

They need to know and feel that they're understood. Responding to them through comforting actions such as a massage does wonders in addressing their emotional needs.

Again, be reminded that they can "anchor" or associate your touch with certain emotions. It's best to be mindful of their emotional state, the type of touch you give, and when you give it, so that you can maximize the benefits of positive touch in your relationship.

Your use of massage and other forms of positive touch to uplift them is particularly important at a time when they are experiencing a variety of stressors unique to their generation. Schools are more uptight, expectations for academic excellence are higher, and the competition among peers are stiffer.

These children, included in what we call Generation Z, also have a unique set of physical woes that massage can address.

The Power Of Positive Touch

Most of those who use their smartphones, iPads, and computers to an excess tend to live sedentary lifestyles and suffer from "tech-necks." Long hours spent on their gadgets also promote poor posture, which can result in strained muscles.

Excessive or not, the majority of today's children tune in to various forms of technological devices more than ever before due to social media and schoolwork. That can have adverse effects on the quality and the duration of their sleep. Spending the half-hour before their bedtime enjoying a gentle massage rather than scrolling through their newsfeed can help them overcome insomnia.

These benefits span certain demographics, too, like children with disabilities or those who've suffered from some form of abuse. These two topics are discussed thoroughly in the latter part of this book, because more than reprieve, touch therapy through massage can provide healing.

Before you Perform Touch Therapies

Paediatric massage is not as simple as you might think it is. The nature of the massages you've enjoyed in your adulthood are most probably not suitable for children.

While there are easy techniques like my recommendation for colic that you can do without training, it's always best to receive expert instruction before using massage to address other conditions.

Remember that children are more fragile and have fewer associations with touch at this stage of their lives. They're just beginning to get to know their preferences and tolerance.

The Power Of Positive Touch

For teachers, foster parents, and orphan keepers, it's especially important to coordinate with the parents, guardians, or government organization looking after the best interest of the children in your care.

The "few associations" they may already have with touch must always come into consideration, even if your incorporation of it in homes or classes are intended for fun and relaxation.

There are many factors involved in providing a truly positive experience of touch through massage therapy. One of the first steps to achieving that is to understand the difference between adult and paediatric massage.

Chapter Three

The 5 P's of Paediatric Massage

Children possess unique wants and needs. Pediatric massage must always take into consideration the physical, mental, emotional, and legal differences between a child and an adult.

One of these differences is the significant growth that children undergo. Depending on where they are in their development, they could still be getting used to a number of physical changes.

These are the years when their skin is thinner, and their sensory receptors are densely packed together.

It's at around the age of twenty-five when all bones in the human body are completely "ossified", meaning they're fully formed. A gentle approach, therefore, is not a preference, but a need.

To give children a massage they'll appreciate and benefit from, you must be careful to mind these five points patterned after *Paediatric Massage: A Massage Therapist's Guide to Getting Started* by Tina Allen.

PERMISSION

Getting a child's permission before you engage in paediatric massage is of utmost importance. You must also make sure that they understand what you intend to do and how it benefits them.

This level of respect communicates their autonomy and right to say no to any physical contact they dislike. If they learn this from you, they'll have the same-if not a higher-standard or boundary for people outside their immediate family or circle.

When asking, explicitly give them the option to say no. Explain to them that they can tell you to stop any time they feel uncomfortable, unsure, or in pain.

Children, especially younger ones, might need time to process this information. They're often made to accept by default that grownups know best. This can make them feel that any stress or discomfort they experience before, during, or after the massage is invalid.

The Power Of Positive Touch

If the children cannot verbalize their consent, simplify your approach by sticking to yes or no questions. Let them respond using gestures such as nodding or shaking their heads.

For parents, you have to know the non-verbal cues your children send that communicate their real feelings about the massage. Any instance of pulling away, shallow breathing, or tensing of the muscles is a sign of aversion or pain. Pay close attention to their body language to determine when to stop a massage.

For teachers who want to incorporate massage in class activities, make sure that you assign each one to a partner of the same gender. The school and the parents must also be informed prior, and any concern raised and addressed before implementation.

Teachers caring for special needs children do well to exercise an even higher level of caution and cooperation with parents. You have to be well-informed of each child's likes and dislikes. Take note of their typical behaviour when they're averted to certain things. This may mean introducing massage slowly and letting them get accustomed to it at their own pace.

PACE

Children, when they are in perfect health, may find it challenging to stay still for long periods of time. If they have a medical condition, a lengthy massage session can be a burden on their weakened body.

A fifteen to twenty-minute massage session is great for most children with short attention spans. You can also give multiple short massage sessions throughout the day.

Similar to aforementioned points, pay attention to their non-verbal cues. Regularly remind them that they can be honest with you so that you'll know whether they want to stop or continue.

Children's moods and preferences can vary from one day to another. It shouldn't come as a surprise if they dislike today the twenty-minute massage they enjoyed yesterday. Include them in the decision-making for each session and respect their choices. Forcing it on them can lead to unpleasant associations with massage.

PRESSURE

The amount of pressure you should use in paediatric massage has no set rule. A firm touch can feel comfortable to one child and painful to another. An older child may find light pressure to be soothing. A younger, ticklish child, however, may find it unbearable. Do your best to meet the needs of every child in each session accordingly.

It's essential to allow children to control the amount of pressure for their massage. Be ready for them to test this control by checking if you will comply with their requests. You need to build trust with each child because it's crucial to their experience.

As they grow older, they can develop better tolerance to pressure, and their ticklish tendencies could wane. Any injury or condition must always be part of the consideration, too, because they might need something different from what they're used to.

The Power Of Positive Touch

It's totally fine if you spend an entire session just building trust. Once you've established your rapport and gained their confidence, the children can relax and benefit from the massage.

POSITIONING

A comfortable position for an adult can be uncomfortable for a child. In some cases where a child is attached to medical equipment or suffers from chronic pain, changing sides can be difficult. Lying on the stomach might even be impossible.

Try different positions such as supine, semi-reclined, or supported side lying. If they say they prefer to stand or to sit, then accommodate their request.

In fact, these alternatives prove to be advantageous in paediatric massage. They enable you to maintain eye contact with the children and observe their facial expressions. At any point that you sense they're uncomfortable but are hesitant to tell you, you can pause and encourage them to speak up.

Another important point you have to remember is that child massage is done clothed.

Parents may share a level of comfort with their children that makes it okay to remove certain articles of clothing. Remember, though, that this must also be done with permission. Parents need to respect their children's decision to not show skin, even if they're family.

The Power Of Positive Touch

School activities involving massage must never encourage the removal of any clothing whatsoever. If some children prefer to keep their jackets or sweaters on, then everybody must respect that. It's also helpful to have them seated, as that's a good way for any teacher to monitor their response to the massage.

Another point for positioning we need to tackle is the placing of the hands. Just as a professional masseuse should never touch erogenous areas, neither should any parent or teacher.

Discuss with them which body parts they'd like for you to massage. The foremost parts where muscles tense are the shoulders, backs, arms, lower legs, and feet. Make sure that they understand this, as well as the result they can expect.

Teachers must be vigilant during classroom activities, as children might overstep their bounds. They might do it with the notion that they're just joking or pulling a prank. Don't let them engage in any activity that involves prolonged touching if they can't fully grasp the concept of personal boundary.

PARENTS

This final point is primarily for teachers who serve as secondary parents to the children at school.

Regardless if a child is in perfect health or is a patient with depleted energy levels, caring for them can be scary. Parents and teachers alike tend to feel pressured to always make the right decisions. This is why it's essential for both parties to coordinate when employing methods like paediatric massage.

The Power Of Positive Touch

Bear in mind that it's the parents or the primary guardian who have the ultimate say on the participation of their children in any massage activity. When you're successful in coordinating these school activities with them, you increase the children's chances of creating healthy associations with touch.

You can start with something simple like five-minute shoulder rubs before classes. Make sure to demonstrate the activity first and to explain its purpose. In every classroom activity that involves touch, you have to be keen in your supervision to ensure that everybody has a great time.

Where classroom massage activities are not allowed, you can instead equip parents to do it at home.

If you're a teacher with knowledge and experience in paediatric massage, teach parents simple techniques. Recommend books and local masseuse they can learn from and share what you know about the benefits of positive touch.

You can even lend them this book. It serves as a good source of foundational knowledge on paediatric massage for non-practitioners.

Remember these 5 P's whenever you massage children. They're the fundamental guidelines that will enable you to give them a positive experience.

The Power Of Positive Touch

While these apply to children from different backgrounds and health conditions, it takes a deeper understanding of their individual cases for you to possibly achieve healing or, at the least, bring them closer to attaining it.

Marija Kisieliene

Chapter Four

Positive Touch Through Massage for Children with Special Needs

Children with special needs require a different level of care from the people around them. Parents and teachers alike bear the responsibility to be the first to give them this special kind of care.

It came as no surprise to me that the teacher I mentioned in my introductory chapter gave such high importance to her ability to pick up a five-year-old boy with autism.

The Power Of Positive Touch

It's that kind of devotion that these children need, especially in the early stages of their development.

Depending on their condition and their unique circumstances, children with special needs can be challenging to manage. You'll need the right knowledge and methods for your efforts to truly impact them.

Massage is an excellent and accessible means for you to manage the tricky aspects of their conditions. Attributes like hyperactivity, short attention spans, and even a natural dislike for physical touch can be addressed better through massage. This is because it is, among other things, an approach that communicates your empathy for them, and fortifies feelings of love and security through positive touch.

With the use of the 5 P's, as well as the rest of the knowledge and instructions shared throughout this book, massage can take its place as a leading tool for enhancing their quality of life.

To better understand how, I've compiled a list of its benefits on some of the most common special needs conditions and disorders.

AUTISM

Autism spectrum disorder or ASD is a developmental condition. People diagnosed with it usually have trouble with communication and social interactions. They don't adapt well to change and are often restricted to routines and repetition, both in food preference and speech patterns. You'll also notice that their reactivity to sound, touch, and scents can often be classified as either hypersensitive or hyposensitive.

Research shows that massage intervention can promote increased levels of on-task and social relatedness behaviour during play. After a session, they also tend to demonstrate low levels of erratic behaviour and increased levels of attentiveness.

Children with autism are among those with special needs who have an innate aversion to physical touch. Researchers at the University of Haifa in Israel conducted a study that revealed the difference between the response of neurotypical people and ASD-diagnosed individuals when it comes to physical contact.

Brain scans showed that the latter, when touched, have a physiological reaction similar to that of a person reacting due to phobia.

The nurturing and safe touch used in massage, combined with consistent sensory integration, help reduce inattentiveness, withdrawal, and fear of touch.

It's an approach that will take time for them to get used to, but with due coordination and consideration for each child, it's possible to achieve these results.

Tactile stimulation through massage can also promote body awareness and, when incorporated in their daily routine, better sleep.

ADHD

Attention deficit hyperactivity disorder or ADHD is a medical condition associated with brain development. Children with ADHD find it more challenging than other children to sit still, pay attention, or finish a task. They can also be impulsive, fidgety, and excessively talkative.

Temper flare-ups is another common attribute they share. They typically have a hard time expressing their emotions, and their sensitive nature can make stressful situations culminate in angry outbursts.

Massage helps by boosting their serotonin and dopamine levels to induce calm. Along with relaxing their muscles, producing endorphins, and lowering heart and blood pressure, massage aids in improving their mood and social functioning. They'll also feel more focused and composed at the end of each session, which can help them deal better with school activities and house chores.

Epilepsy

Epilepsy is a seizure disorder that can have an unknown cause. It's commonly characterized by black outs, convulsions, and frothing in the mouth. These episodes may lead to injury if they're not effectively managed.

The primary way that massage helps with epilepsy is by reducing the tenderness that children feel due to the violent muscle contractions they experience during a seizure.

Since an episode is commonly followed by feelings of embarrassment, helplessness, and confusion, giving them a massage can help them deal with these stressful emotions. The better they manage their stress, the better they'll cope with their condition.

They'll also benefit from improved sleep, which is invaluable to their condition. Sleep deprivation can trigger their seizures, so massaging them before bedtime will prove to be a good addition to your night-time routine.

Down Syndrome

Down syndrome is a common genetic birth condition. Some of the health problems they experience are hypotonia, heart disease, seizures, spinal cord compression, and constipation.

Regular massage can help improve their muscle tone, motor skills, language skills, and relieve constipation. Since no case of Down syndrome is exactly the same, it's important for a professional to have access to their full history before performing a massage.

This is one of the conditions in which expert treatment and advice is critical, because any amateur attempt at massage can have serious risks. It's especially true for children with cardiac problems, as well as atlanto-axial instability. If parents or teachers are to do this, they must consult first with a certified massage therapist and learn techniques from them.

Cerebral Palsy

Cerebral palsy is a result of brain injury that is incurred during pregnancy, at childbirth, or within infancy and early childhood. It commonly affects children's muscle tone and motor skills, along with body functions such as breathing, eating, and bowel control. Depending on the type and severity of the brain damage they incur, it can also cause problems with their vision, speech, and hearing.

Children with cerebral palsy who receive massage have lower levels of spasticity, reduced rigidity in muscle tone, and enhanced gross and fine motor functions. Moreover, the developmental profile of children who receive massage show better social and dressing scores. They exhibit reduced limb activity during face-to-face play interactions, and more positive facial expressions.

Educating Yourself

While I'm a licenced massage therapist, my descriptions of these conditions, as well as the benefits of massage that I listed, should not be considered medical advice.

Bear in mind that each child has a unique medical history and set of circumstances that need to be considered in order to make massage beneficial.

True, lasting benefits come from an educated application of massage to children. It's always best to partner with professionals such as a certified masseuse to ensure that the treatment stays safe, pleasurable, and efficient for the children.

I encourage you to keep learning through whatever means you can and to use this book as a reference to your endeavours in soothing and improving your child's condition.

If you're interested in signing up for my classes or enlisting my services, you can reach out to me through my website and social media, which you'll find at the end of this book. I'm always more than willing to use my expertise to assist anyone with the heart to help children through positive touch.

For parents, you can sit in during a massage session with your child so that I can explain everything that I do. Afterwards, I will give you instructions on how you can massage them at home.

For teachers who feel their students will benefit from positive touch in the classroom, I would be happy to go to your school and educate your entire faculty on the right way to do it. I have training courses that we can customize to meet your specific goals and requirements.

I stand by the famous African proverb that says, "It takes a village to raise a child."

Marija Kisieliene

We are a community of parents and teachers with a lot of responsibility on our hands. It should be our common goal to come together and do everything we can to raise healthy, safe, and happy children.

Chapter Five

Massage for Underserved and Abused Children

Positive touch through massage is both challenging and fulfilling when applied to the underserved and abused demographic of children.

It's challenging because you're introducing touch to them in a way they have never experienced before, and this can be scary for them.

You'll have to take into consideration many things, including their personal history, health record, and overall well-being. Each child is a different case, which means your methods should cater to their unique needs, and that's not always an easy task.

On the other hand, it's fulfilling because you're playing an active part in their healing. The earlier you address their issues with neglect and abuse, the easier it will be to improve their quality of life now and in the future.

To make a true and lasting difference for these children, you have to understand where they're coming from in terms of touch deprivation and trauma.

Understanding Underserved Populations

Children who live in orphanages and foster homes across the world might be getting food, clothing, and shelter, but often they don't receive one of the most important components of health and happiness, which is *positive touch*.

It's difficult for these units to meet the essential developmental needs of children through personalized attention and care. This leaves the majority of them feeling as though they're insignificant and unwanted.

If you're a foster parent or are somehow involved in the care of children in these situations, you'll know that most of them are tough to bond with. You've probably encountered some who've been transferring from home to home since they were six, or runaways who keep getting pulled back into the system.

It doesn't help that they also suffer from the stress that comes with the trauma and stigma of being either abandoned by their parents or removed by the state from their homes. Even when they successfully undergo adoption, they can still struggle with abandonment issues that may endure throughout their lifetime.

Depending on where you are in the world, the system for both types of care can have varying effects on these children.

This is especially true in foster homes, because while there are families who do this out of the goodness of their hearts, there are also those who are motivated by the monetary incentives provided by the government.

When these homes go unchecked and their treatment of these children are overlooked, they become breeding grounds for another serious problem, which is abuse.

Understanding Abused Children

When adults put children in risky situations, ignore their needs, involve them in anything sexual, and degrade them either through words or actions, that's considered abuse.

Another important point you need to understand is that not all children in this denomination come from orphanages and foster homes. Child abuse also isn't unique to families in poverty.

It can happen to anyone from any socioeconomic, religious, and racial background.

Some, like myself, have grown up with parents who have also been mistreated, and they don't know any other way of parenting. The scars this creates can be passed down from generation to generation unless someone intervenes, or the abuse survivors decide they will not turn into their abusers.

The effects of maltreating and violating children can be so grave that it becomes the sole determinant for their self-respect, their relationships, their ambitions, and every other area of their lives.

They may develop an intolerance for personal attachments, and even touch. They can have trouble allowing people into their personal space, and manifest knee-jerk reactions that even they can't explain.

This is especially true for those who suffer physical and sexual abuse. These children have had inappropriate and unwanted contact from someone with the intention to exhibit power, control, violence, intimidation, and rage using sex.

The Power Of Positive Touch

Sexual abuse is traumatic, regardless of how it is inflicted. It violates the victim's integrity on so many levels. It leaves deep and lasting effects on the emotional and psychological functioning of abuse survivors.

Moreover, those who suffer prolonged abuse in their childhood do not have any reliable measure to judge who they can trust and what situations are safe.

Since their physical, emotional, and sexual boundaries have been violated, they also often have trouble defining boundaries in relationships, which puts them at risk of even more abuse.

The Role of Massage Therapy in Healing

Massage therapy is beneficial in creating a healing environment for abuse survivors; however, it's crucial for you to be sensitive about their experiences and how they can affect your massage sessions.

There's a chance you could be the first person to give them positive touch after their abusive encounter. This puts a lot of weight on your shoulders to make their massage a positive experience, as opposed to a trigger to their trauma.

While an amateur and inconsiderate attempt at massage can potentially induce feelings of fear and confusion, the correct approach can re-introduce their sense of self and help them feel grounded, safe, and in charge.

The Power Of Positive Touch

Regardless of your expertise, however, there's no telling when even a simple touch can trigger intense emotions and unexpected reactions. It's vital to know how to recognize and manage these kinds of instances so that they don't hinder massage from contributing to these children's healing.

Again, while massage in itself is not a cure, it does address numerous issues that can complement other forms of therapy.

Among these issues are repression as a defence mechanism and dissociative numbing, where the child temporarily disconnects from their bodies and their environment as a means to cope.

Since the body is a direct medium, massage can promote the re-entry process and help them feel more present.

Being able to show love and appreciation to themselves-particularly to their bodies-is a huge leap towards recovery. Their abuse could've given them feelings of disgust and shame. Unaddressed, these may even result in self-harm as a means to relieve themselves of such emotions.

Helping children deal with all these negative associations and poor means of coping with their trauma will help them lead better lives as adults. They'll be more open to trusting other people again, therefore increasing their chances of building authentic attachments throughout their lives.

Trained massage therapists can provide nonsexual and non-abusive touch to these children, creating a safe place for them to reconnect with their physical selves. With sufficient instruction, you can also massage them in a way that will help them reclaim control of their bodies. Each session gives them an avenue to exercise their right to choose where and when they are comfortable to be touched.

When you comply with their request to decrease or increase the pressure, or to not touch them in certain body parts, you're helping them build essential boundaries. This improves their sense of control because it lets them understand that they have the authority to accept and refuse someone's touch. Just being able to say "no" and "stop" is empowering for an abuse survivor.

Their experience with massage as a non-sexual touch that can either be neutral or pleasurable also impacts their healing. It helps them untangle negative associations with touch that typically leaves them feeling numb or empty.

Aligned with the three stages of recovery described by American psychiatrist Judith Lewis Herman, you can enhance these children's positive experience with massage and amplify its benefits.

The 3 Stages of Recovery

Some clinicians claim that recovery from trauma has stages, while others contend that healing is more of a fluid process without any definitive structure.

Although the healing process might be a continuum, the three stages of recovery mentioned by Judith Lewis Herman in her book *Trauma and Recovery: The Aftermath of Violence - From Domestic Abuse to Political Terror* can help you work better with abuse survivors.

They will give you an idea of where children stand in terms of recovery, even though they might go back and forth stages two and three or experience both at the same time.

Establishing Safety

The aim of the first stage is to establish psychological and physical safety. This is when survivors learn to take control of their bodies and address their physical needs, such as eating, sleeping, exercising, and living in a safe environment. This immediate sense of safety helps them take the initiative to pursue their recovery.

This stage can last from a few sessions to a few years, depending on the individual and the circumstances of their trauma.

Remembrance and Mourning

When a survivor establishes safety, their previously buried, disguised, fragmented, or unconscious memories become conscious. They can then reconstruct them as vital pieces of their life story.

Remembrance and mourning have the tendency to be long and deeply painful. As survivors go through the horrors and aches of their traumas, they also have to come to terms with the loss and grief they've suffered but have yet to express. It's by retelling their story and processing all the negative emotions associated with them that they can heal and move forward.

Reconnection

Reconnection is when survivors start to develop a complete and intact sense of self that can entertain thoughts of the future. They recognize their trauma but are not possessed by it. It's at this stage that their confidence increases and they're better able to connect with the world. They maintain a level of certainty in their decisions to give and withhold trust, and they can interact with people on their own terms.

This is the third and final stage of recovery. While abuse survivors may repeatedly experience Remembrance and Mourning, it eventually gets easier for them to move forward and fully reconnect with themselves and with society.

The Significance of Psychotherapy in Recovery

Those who don't have a background in psychology or have never worked with abuse survivors before might not be able to identify where they are in their recovery. This is why I recommend that these children take other forms of therapy as well.

If you've visited a psychotherapist prior to reading this book, you might've already received a recommendation to use massage on abuse survivors as a support to traditional counselling.

While psychotherapy works with the conscious mind, massage works with the body to help the child collect information from the subconscious mind. The physicality of massage gives them a heightened awareness of the repressed memories and emotions that they need to deal with.

When you coordinate with a psychotherapist, he or she may suggest that you (if you've received sufficient training and instruction) or a certified masseuse give children a massage before they undergo talking therapy. This is because a counselling session conducted after a massage can result in better cognitive connections with them.

Massage also lowers the characteristic resistance in survivors and makes them more present for therapeutic insight.

The advantage of complementing one therapy with another is that they meet more of the children's needs.

Each kind of therapy has its limitations in terms of specialty, which means it only treats part of the problem. That won't suffice in dealing with abuse, especially of the physical and sexual nature, because there's more to children than the mental and emotional scars they incur. In the same way, there's also more to their trauma than their visible bruises, injuries, and reactivity.

More than just obtaining knowledge and instruction about massage for abuse survivors, you should coordinate with professionals to create the best plan of treatment for the children under your care.

In the next chapter, we'll go into more detail about the precautions you should take before massaging abuse survivors.

Chapter Six

Preparation for Massaging Abuse Survivors

Pursue adequate preparation before massaging the children in your care, especially if they're abuse survivors.

You don't need to earn a certification or a license to use positive touch to help them heal. What you need as a parent or as a teacher is proper instruction to avoid bringing them more harm than good.

When it comes to abuse survivors, you must understand that you can't take their recovery into your own hands unless you have the education and experience to do so.

Coordinate with professionals like me and other reputable people in the field of therapy to create a personalized plan for each child.

Choose a certified masseuse who has treated abuse survivors before, especially young children. Coordinate with him or her about massage techniques you can learn and perform at home, if any. You may receive advice against it depending on the child's state. If you do, know that it's for the best. Your masseuse will allow you to perform massage at home when you and the child are both ready for it.

The Power Of Positive Touch

One of the primary goals of getting coached is to give you the confidence to provide positive touch. It's when you're sure about your approach and the relief you're bringing into an abuse survivor's life that your actions truly become substantive to them.

One chapter won't suffice to give you all the instructions you'll need to gain that level of preparedness. What I aim to do is to give you an idea of where to start, what to do, and how you can do it.

I'll discuss with you six points that will serve as the foundation of your knowledge when it comes to helping abuse survivors through massage.

Psychological Understanding

Talk to a psychologist. Reach out to me and to other incredible masseuses who've provided this specific treatment before. Read as many books as you can about abuse survivors and their individual journeys to recovery. Find credible websites with stories of how parents, teachers, and other people helped another person heal from abuse.

With today's technology and the level of convenience it brings, you can get almost any kind of resource on your smartphone or delivered to your doorstep at any time.

Tackle subjects about the healing process such as power differentials, boundary issues, body memory, transference, and countertransference. You'll also want to know more about the different types of abuse and their effects on children.

A well-rounded perspective on abuse can improve your relationship with the survivor and with the therapists who will be involved in the treatment.

Workshops and Training

When signing up for classes, always start with the basics and build up your knowledge from there. Practice what you learn on yourself or with family and friends who can support you in this endeavour.

It's rare to find courses on treatment for abuse survivors that are available to non-practitioners. This could mean you'll have to get one-on-one coaching from a professional who's willing to help. In some cases, the masseuse treating your child may initiate it for continued treatment at home.

Marija Kisieliene

Massage for abuse survivors are not as complex or physically challenging as the ones you get for leisure. The real challenge you'll face will be on an emotional and mental level.

Look for workshops or seminars that will educate you on how to set up the right environment at home. Equip yourself with the knowledge on how to deal with dissociation and flashbacks. Listen to talks about communication, particularly on the subject of abuse, so that you can recognize the non-verbal cues of your child.

When you're able to establish good communication between the two of you, you create a collaboration that is empowering and non-hierarchical. Those two things are crucial for a survivor's healing.

Allow them to feel a sense of control over their recovery. Do what you can to validate their autonomy, because they might have lost both in the hands of their abusers.

Motivations and Issues

You want to help children who are abuse survivors-that's a given. The real question, then, is this: Why?

Try to go beyond reasons of moral obligation to identify any personal motivation you may have for your actions. Do you know someone who was abused and never recovered? Have you witnessed the neglect and maltreatment of children before, and it has impacted you in such a powerful way that it moved you into action?

Perhaps you're an abuse survivor yourself.

It's important to deal with these deeper personal reasons because they have the potential to negatively affect your efforts to help these children. If you've suffered abuse in the past but haven't healed from it, you'll want to work on your recovery first.

Sign up for psychotherapy to develop an understanding of your own hurts and unmet needs. Other personal reasons like witnessing a sibling or a friend getting abused can also be traumatic and warrants healing.

Even when you're the one giving the massage, it can still evoke many strong feelings that won't benefit your child to witness.

I encourage you to take good care of yourself too. You are valuable and deserving of love and respect. When your children see you embrace your worth, it's easier for them to embrace theirs.

Ethical Dimensions

When massage is done for abuse survivors, the importance of ethical dimensions intensifies. There must be a well-thought-out ethical code that the masseuse should stick to, and which you should be fully aware of.

It must be clear to you how a practitioner should behave with the child during the treatment. For instance, a masseuse would normally recommend treating children of the same gender.

They should never require the children to remove all their clothing or prohibit any parent or guardian from staying in the same room during the massage.

Depending on where you live, massage therapy might not be a properly regulated industry. Some unqualified individuals may claim the title of therapist without worry of any official institution to hold them accountable for it.

If you're unsure of the masseuse or the clinic you want to visit, ask for government-issued clearances and certificates. A true professional masseuse wouldn't shy away from inquiries about their education and certifications as well. It's your right to know, and your job to make sure that your children are safe in their hands.

Support and Supervision

Abuse is a sensitive topic, and you should respect the survivor's decision for confidentiality even from close family members. Being a child does not invalidate their desire to keep their issues private.

Any information you think you must share with anyone else, you have to first let the child know and permit. Bypassing them and later getting caught will cause distrust, and that's a major roadblock to their healing process. It will send a message that if they can't trust their parents or primary caregivers, they cannot trust anybody else, least of all strangers.

Be prepared to explain difficult things to them on a level that they'll understand, and to do so many times until they fully grasp them.

Instead of walking them into therapy without prior notice, consult the idea with them weeks before. Tell them why you think it will help, and how. Wait for them to warm up to the idea of therapy at their own pace instead of forcing it on them.

The same applies to massage and to the other approaches you'll try.

The more willing and attuned they are to their own healing, the better their chances of succeeding at it.

Preparing to help abuse survivors can be a laborious process. Remember that you don't have to do it alone. Collaborate with the survivors themselves and create a support group that will be part of these children's recovery. Be vigilant in selecting the treatment you choose and the therapists you work with.

The Power Of Positive Touch

I've travelled this road before, and I have a clear picture of what it takes to get to the other side where survivors, along with their parents and teachers, achieve healing and peace.

If it's possible for me and my son, it's possible for you too.

Marija Kisieliene

Final Words

Congratulations. If you've read this far, you've hopefully developed a better understanding of positive touch. It's a tool accessible to any parent and teacher, and I want you to use what you've just learned to improve your children's quality of life.

In the process, I hope it improves yours too.

Positive touch has been integral in my healing as an abuse survivor, and it has proved invaluable in my relationship with my children, particularly my son. I've witnessed its transformative power in the students of the special needs teacher I encountered, and in the children of the parents that I've coached.

The Power Of Positive Touch

I'm filled with awe whenever I treat children with depression, anxiety, or nausea, and I see how a fifteen-minute massage does so much to relieve them. Parents shared with me that the techniques I taught them reduced their children's chronic headaches and led to better sleeping habits.

I've also had the privilege of seeing the children whose parents I've coached in infant massage grow up to be physically, mentally, and emotionally healthy. They've developed strong relationships with their mothers and fathers through regular massage, which gives me the confidence that they'll turn out to be well-rounded adults.

The increasing number of special needs children I treat have also been faring better. The teachers of those diagnosed with autism and ADHD shared with me the increased attentiveness and improved social functioning they observed. Some children with autism had also become less reactive to touch, which is a great accomplishment given their innate aversion to it.

The successes of the parents and teachers I've worked with in the treatment of abuse survivors are among those I'm proudest of. We stood by each other as we helped abused children heal from their visible and invisible bruises. Some journeys took longer than most, but with every session that a child learned to recognize positive touch, we saw the value of our efforts.

If you're a parent, foster parent, or a teacher who wants to make positive touch a part of your children's lives, expect that it's going to change you as well. You're going to have moments of reflection, first about touch, and then about the many ways you can still do better as a significant figure of love and authority to them.

I know that in spite of the changes I've already gone through, and the numerous people I've helped, I'm still growing. Every day, I'm doing things to become the best mother, masseuse, and coach that I can be.

Positive touch is like a butterfly that flaps its wings and causes a typhoon. One small touch and one little action can make your and your children's lives better.

We tackled many things about positive touch through massage, but there's more to its application and benefits than this book can contain. There are stories I have yet to tell you, and insights I still want to discuss.

To find out more about positive touch and my work, visit my website

www.chancetorelaxstoke.co.uk and my Facebook page @chancetorelaxstokeontrent. You can also connect with me on my personal Facebook account Marija Kisieliene or visit my studio, Chance to Relax, in Stoke-on-Trent.

I have instructions and techniques to teach that, when learned and harnessed by a community of parents and teachers, can give many children a safer and happier childhood.

I encourage you to share my vision, and together, we can make a difference.

DEIVIDAI

LINKIU, KAD KIEKVIENAS TAVO PRISILIETIMAS BUTŲ KUPINAS SILUMOS IR GERUMO, NES TEIGIAMI JAUSMAI IR VEIKSMAI VISADA ATNEŠA TEIGEMUS REZULTATUS
SU ŠILČIAUSIAIS LINKĖJIMAIS

: MARIJA : KISIELIENE